The United States

Kentucky

Anne Welsbacher
ABDO & Daughters

visit us at
www.abdopub.com

Published by Abdo & Daughters, 4940 Viking Drive, Suite 622, Edina, Minnesota 55435.
Copyright © 1998 by Abdo Consulting Group, Inc., Pentagon Tower, P.O. Box 36036, Minneapolis, Minnesota 55435 USA. International copyrights reserved in all countries. No part of this book may be reproduced in any form without written permission from the publisher.

Printed in the United States.

Cover and Interior Photo credits: Super Stock, Archive Photos, Corbis-Bettman

Edited by Lori Kinstad Pupeza
Contributing editor Brooke Henderson
Special thanks to our Checkerboard Kids—Jack Ward, Raymond Sherman, Annie O'Leary, Gracie Hansen, Morgan Roberts

All statistics taken from the 1990 census; The Rand McNally Discovery Atlas of The United States. Other sources: *Kentucky*, Fradin, Children's Press, Chicago, 1993; *Kentucky*, McNair, Children's Press, Chicago, 1988; *Kentucky*, Brown, Lerner Publications Co., Minneapolis, 1992; America Online, Compton's Living Encyclopedia, 1997; World Book Encyclopedia, 1990.

Library of Congress Cataloging-in-Publication Data

Welsbacher, Anne, 1955-
    Kentucky / Anne Welsbacher.
    p. cm. -- (United States)
    Includes index.
    Summary: Surveys the history, geography, people, cities, and other aspects of the Bluegrass State.
    ISBN 1-56239-874-1
    1. Kentucky--Juvenile literature. [1. Kentucky.] I. Title. II Series: United States (Series).
    F451.3.W45   1998
    976.9--dc21
                                         97-20593
                                       CIP
                                       AC.

Contents

Welcome to Kentucky

Kentucky has mountains, woodlands, and long caves. It has farms and coal mines. It has horse racing and country music.

Kentucky is in the southern part of the United States. But it is like the north in many ways. Kentuckians fought on both sides of the Civil War!

Kentucky is famous for country music and bluegrass music. Bluegrass is the name of a kind of grass that covers much of Kentucky. So Kentucky is known as the Bluegrass State.

Opposite page: This horse ranch is in the Blue Grass Basin of Kentucky.

Fast Facts

KENTUCKY

Capital
Frankfort (25,968 people)
Area
39,674 square miles
(102,755 sq km)
Population
3,698,969 people
Rank: 23rd
Statehood
June 1, 1792
(15th state admitted)
Principal rivers
Cumberland River, Kentucky
River, Ohio River
Highest point
Black Mountain;
4,139 feet (1,262 m)
Largest city
Louisville (269,063 people)
Motto
United we stand, divided we fall
Song
"My Old Kentucky Home"
Famous People
Muhammad Ali, John James
Audubon, Daniel Boone, Loretta
Lynn, Whitney M. Young,
Cassius Marcellus Clay

*S*tate Flag

*G*oldenrod

*C*ardinal

*K*entucky Coffee Tree

About Kentucky

The Bluegrass State

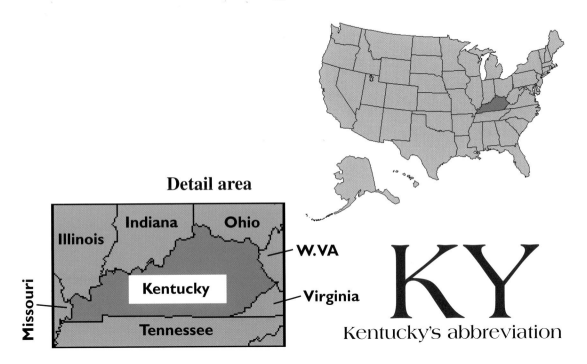

Detail area

KY

Kentucky's abbreviation

Borders: west (Missouri), north (Illinois, Indiana, Ohio), east (W. Virginia, Virginia), south (Tennessee)

Nature's Treasures

Kentucky has coal in much of its land. It has other minerals, too. It has limestone, clay, sand, gravel, and zinc.

Kentucky also has rich soil. Much of it is good for farming. Kentucky is warm and rainy. It rains the most in the spring. It has warm summers and cool winters.

Kentucky has many lakes. Many of the lakes were made by people.

The Cumberland Falls is Kentucky's longest waterfall. It is 68 feet (21 m) long. If you and 16 of your friends stood on top of each other, you could reach the top of the Cumberland Falls!

Opposite page: Cumberland Falls State Park, Kentucky.

Beginnings

Early people came to Kentucky about 11,000 years ago. They buried their dead and covered them with dirt. This made small hills, called mounds. So the people were called Mound Builders. Later, other groups came to Kentucky. Some were called the Woodlands people, Shawnee, Cherokee, and Iroquois people.

In the mid 1700s, Daniel Boone found a path in the Cumberland Mountains. He was the first to go through it. The path was called the Cumberland Pass.

Settlers came from other states. The Shawnee and Cherokee fought with them. But the army forced the Native Americans out of Kentucky. In 1792, Kentucky became the 15th state. Slaves were forced to work on Kentucky farms. They grew corn and tobacco.

In the 1860s, northern states did not want slavery to continue. But the southern states still wanted slavery.

Many southern states **seceded** from the United States. This led to the Civil War.

Kentucky was **divided**. Kentucky sided with the North. Most Kentuckians fought for the North. But some fought for the South.

The North won the Civil War. In the 1870s, the North tried to help the South rebuild. This was called **Reconstruction**. Then the North stopped helping the South.

African Americans were no longer slaves. But they still did not have the same rights as white people. Even into the mid-1900s, many white people would not hire black people or sell them houses.

Daniel Boone

In the 1950s and 1960s, the **Civil Rights movement** was born. People walked in marches and worked to make new laws. In 1968, Kentucky became the first southern state to pass a Civil Rights law.

B.C. to 1650s

Early Kentucky

 11,000 B.C.-2500 B.C.: People travel to Kentucky, settle, and build mounds.

 1500-1600: The Mound Builders disappear. The Woodlands people live in Kentucky.

 1650s: Among the people in Kentucky are the Shawnee, Cherokee, Delaware, and Iroquois people.

1700 to 1800

Through the Cumberland Pass

 1700s: Settlers from nearby states cross the Appalachian mountains. Many of them have families who came to America from Scotland and Ireland. They bring with them their music and dance traditions.

 1792: Kentucky becomes a state.

 1800: Shawnee and other Native Americans are forced west and south of Kentucky. Settlers bring slaves.

1861 to Today

Moving with the Times

 1861-1865: Civil War pits the North against the South. Kentucky votes to stay with the North.

 1920s-1950s: Many Kentuckians mine coal instead of farming and hunting.

 1950s-1960s: The **Civil Rights movement** is born.

 1980s: Kentucky works to fix harm done to the land by strip mining.

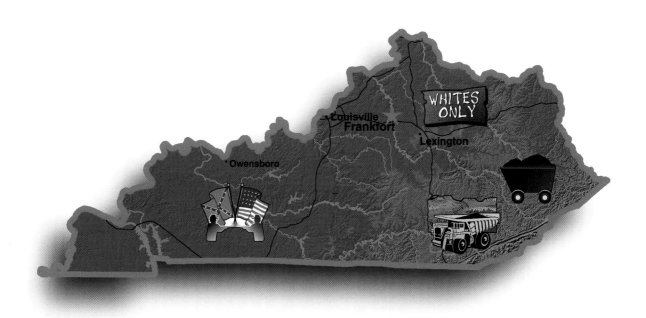

17

Kentucky's People

Kentucky was a farm state for a long time. In the 1900s, many Kentuckians fished for, grew, and hunted all the food they ate.

Later, Kentuckians moved to cities. Today, about one out of every two Kentuckians live in cities.

Country music singer Loretta Lynn and her sister Crystal Gayle are from Kentucky. Jazz music man Lionel Hampton was born in Louisville, Kentucky. He played the "vibraphone"!

The writer Robert Penn Warren was from Guthrie, Kentucky. In 1986, he became the country's first **poet laureate**.

The boxer Muhammad Ali was born in Louisville. Colonel Harland Sanders, from Corbin, Kentucky, invented Kentucky Fried Chicken!

Other Kentucky-born people are Mary Breckinridge, the famous nurse who started the nursing service in rural Kentucky; Cassius Marcellus Clay, who fought slavery; and children's book writer George Ella Lyon.

Muhammad Ali

Cassius Marcellus Clay

Loretta Lynn

Kentucky's Cities

The largest city in Kentucky is Louisville. It is along the Ohio River. Many boats come and go.

Lexington is the next largest city. It has pretty bluegrass, horse farms, and a big **college**.

Frankfort is the capital of Kentucky. Other cities in Kentucky are Owensboro, Hopkinsville, and Bowling Green.

Opposite page:
Louisville, Kentucky.

Kentucky's Land

Kentucky is one of the southern states. But it is very close to the northern part of the United States.

To the north are Indiana and Ohio. To the east are West Virginia and Virginia. To the south is Tennessee. To the west is Missouri. Northwest of Kentucky is Illinois.

Kentucky is shaped like a pile of mashed potatoes! The Ohio River runs along the north border. The Kentucky River cuts through the state. On a map they look like butter and gravy on top of the potatoes!

To the east, Kentucky has very pretty mountains. They are in the Appalachian Plateau. The northern part of the state is the bluegrass area. In the far southwest is swampy land.

Forests fill half of the state. Ash, hickory, oak, maple, and hemlock are some of the trees in Kentucky. Many pretty flowers and plants are magnolias, blueberries, huckleberries, wild plums, jack-in-the-pulpit, buttercups, daisies, Pennyroyals, and bluegrass.

Kentucky animals are foxes, woodchucks, and muskrats. Flying above Kentucky are cardinals, egrets, blue herons, doves, wild ducks, wild geese, barn owls, and woodpeckers. And Kentucky waters have more than 200 kinds of fish!

Mammoth Cave in Kentucky.

Kentucky at Play

Kentuckians love horse racing. The Kentucky Derby is an **annual** spring race held in Louisville. The Kentucky Derby is more than 100 years old!

Kentucky is the land of "bluegrass" music. Bluegrass is played on banjos, harmonicas, and violins (called fiddles). It blends sounds of Scotland and Ireland, where some families of early Kentuckians once lived.

Mammoth Cave National Park, near Louisville, has the world's longest group of caves. It is 300 miles (483 km) long! Near Mammoth Cave is the log cabin where President Abraham Lincoln was born.

The famous Actors Theatre is in Louisville. It has an annual festival of new plays. There also is a famous art museum and orchestra in Louisville. An orchestra is a group of violins, flutes, drums, trumpets, and many other musical instruments.

Kentucky has many state parks. Cumberland Falls is nicknamed the Niagara of the south. That is because there is a big waterfall in the north called Niagara.

You also can see "moonbows" at Cumberland Falls. When there is a full moon, its light makes rainbow colors in the water that splashes from the falls. This is the only place on this side of the planet where you can see a moonbow!

Kentuckians love horses.

Kentucky at Work

Most Kentuckians work in the service industry. Service is selling food, working in hotels, in hospitals, and restaurants, among other things.

Some Kentuckians still mine coal. Others are in **manufacturing**.

Kentuckians make tractors, trucks, paint, and other things.

Kentucky farmers grow tobacco, soybeans, corn, and wheat. They raise horses. They grow peaches and apples. They even grow corn that's used for popcorn!

Opposite page: These barges are moving gravel through Louisville, Kentucky.

Fun Facts

•Both the leaders of the two sides in the Civil War were born in Kentucky! President Abraham Lincoln and Jefferson Davis, who was president of the southern states when they **seceded** from the United States, were born only a few miles away from each other.

•The first cheeseburger in the United States was eaten in Louisville, Kentucky, in 1934.

•Fort Knox, Kentucky, has more gold stored in its vaults than any other place in the world. Almost all the gold owned by the United States is at Fort Knox.

•The first oil well in the world was built in Kentucky in 1829.

•Kentucky grows more burley tobacco (a special kind of tobacco) than anywhere else in the world. And it has held this record for more than 100 years!

- The Kentucky Derby is the oldest horse race in the country. It began in 1875.
- The name "Kentucky" comes from the Cherokee word Ken-tah-teh. Ken-tah-teh might mean "land of tomorrow." Or it might mean "meadow land." Nobody knows for sure.
- Pioneer Daniel Boone wanted to go to Kentucky because it had lots of room and not too many people. He called it "elbow room!"

Horses running at the Kentucky Derby.

Glossary

Annual: happening once every year.

College: a school that people go to after finishing high school.

Divided: to have different beliefs about something.

Civil Rights movement: a time in the 1950s and 1960s when people fought for equal rights for African Americans.

Equal: the same.

Manufacture: to make things.

Poet Laureate: a special honor for poets who write very well.

Reconstruction: a time in American history following the Civil War. The North helped the South rebuild their houses, land, and jobs.

Secede: to break away, to leave a group.

Internet Sites

Kentucky Information Page
http://www.louisville.edu/~easchn01
Contains data and search tools for getting information about Kentucky, the USA, and the World.

Kentucky Tourism Council
http://www.tourky.com
This site shows tourists where to go, what to do, where to stay, and where to eat in Kentucky.

These sites are subject to change. Go to your favorite search engine and type in Kentucky for more sites.

PASS IT ON

Tell Others Something Special About Your State

To educate readers around the country, pass on interesting tips, places to see, history, and little unknown facts about the state you live in. We want to hear from you!

To get posted on ABDO & Daughters website E-mail us at "mystate@abdopub.com"

Index